Run to the Pain

by Robert L. Evans III

PhD, LCPC, LPC, MAC, NCC

Copyright 2020 Robert L. Evans All right reserved.

This book or parts thereof may not be reproduced in any form, stored in any retrieval system, or transmitted in any form by any means — electronic, mechanical, photocopy, recording, or otherwise — without prior written permission of the publisher, except as provided by United States of America copyright law. For permission requests, write to the publisher, at admin@empowertoday.net.

For further information visit the author's website at www.empowertoday.net

Table of Contents

Dedication

Foreword *by Dr. Willie Jolley*

Preface

Introduction

Chapter I Pain

  How Do We Know Pain is Pain?

  Running Away from Physical Pain

    The 5-Second Rule

  Running Away from Emotional Pain

    The 5-Star Process

      Step #1 Allow yourself to release

      Step #2 Identify where to direct your emotions

      Step #3 Accept what can and cannot be changed

      Step #4 Record lessons learned

      Step #5 Continue with daily activities

  Running Away from Psychological Pain

    Ignorance

    Disinformation

    Fear

Chapter II Conditioning

  Self-Awareness

Desire

Intentionality

Emotions

Distorted Thinking

Mental Realignment

Thought Replacement

Chapter III Adversity

Waves

Attitude

Faith

Chapter IV Reconditioning

Adversity's Role

The Blessing of Adversity

Better than Amazingly Designed

Chapter V Learning Lessons

Humility

Motivation

Resiliency

Chapter VI Running Towards the Pain

Processing the Pain in a Healthy Way

The Secret Ingredient to Healing from Pain (Quickly)

Forgiveness

Step #1 Understand the Purpose of Forgiveness

Step #2 Identify Who to Forgive

  Forgiveness of Self

    Acknowledge

    Make Amends

    Make Corrections

  Forgiveness of God

    Seek

    Listen

    Be Ready

Step #3 Understand the Reason for Forgiveness

  Forgive to Let Go

  Forgive to Maintain a Relationship

  Chains of Ignorance

  Chains of Pride

Step #4 Decide

Step #5 Let Go

Chapter VII Universal Law

Acknowledgements

References

Dedication

This book is dedicated to my first hero and father Robert L. Evans, Jr. You have been the single most influential person in shaping me into the man that I am today. As an African American male in American culture and growing up in Washington, DC and Fort Washington, Maryland, having my father in the home and taking care of his family was crucial to my development and view of the family unit. You were the epitome of hard work and responsibility. You may not have realized it, but something as simple as being there to love and take care of my mother as a husband should, had a massive butterfly effect, which allowed me to be free to live my life and pursue my dreams. Being concerned about the wellbeing of my mother was never an issue for me, and that is one of the best gifts a son could ask for. You were always my biggest fan in every sport and you were always present. I never had to think twice or doubt your intentions or question if my needs were going to be met. I didn't get everything I wanted, but I sure got everything I needed.

You raised me in a "children are to be seen and not heard" era. You lectured and talked my head off every day.

And all day. After you finished, then it was the same thing the next day. And during the conversations, I may have spoken one or two words at best. But mostly I was silent. You asked questions and then answered them yourself. You asked my opinion and then gave me my opinion. Sometimes, you were wrong about your impression of what I was thinking, and I just let you think it. It wasn't until some point in high school when you started to realize who I was. What I didn't know then, was that you were preparing me to be one of the best listeners on earth! Although this was not the best communication strategy to build a rapport and promote dialogue, it sculpted my ability to be able to listen quietly and attentively. I truly believe I am a halfway-decent therapist today because of you.

I know you were doing the best you could with the cards you were dealt. Despite your imperfections, you balanced them with consistency, support, positive affirmations, and love. I don't have to tell you to pat yourself on the back, because you take care of that pretty well. This time, I will let you know, you are the greatest of all time! And not for having impeccable techniques, but for having a bulletproof heart! Your work has paid off in dividends because my younger brother Michael Evans and my sister Jennifer Evans, are beyond outstanding individuals as well. Your legacy is solidified! I sincerely thank you for all of your sacrifices and everything you have done for our family! Salute King!

Foreword

Pain is something most people would choose to avoid in life, yet pain is one of the most powerful forces that will ultimately determine your success or failure. Pain is considered one of the driving forces of motivation, along with the forces of pleasure, inspiration, and desperation. The word motivation is taken from the Latin root word *motere* which means that which moves you to take action.

Dr. Robert Evans shares a new perspective about motivation. He explains the power of running to pain rather than always running away from it. In his insightful new book, *Run to the Pain*, he shares that we often miss the powerful lessons which can come as a result of recognizing that pain is a real force for transformation. We as humans often must go through the pain to get to the great opportunities on the other side.

I have personally learned first-hand that this is true. I have experienced life's transformational impact by seeing how pain motivated me to change my thinking and in turn, to change my life.

My life changed one night over thirty years ago, after performing my act at a popular nightclub. The owner told me that while he loved my performance, he wanted to get a better ROI (Return on Investment). He told me he had bought a karaoke machine which was filling up nightclubs at that time. So, he was going to let me go!

I was shocked, hurt, and in great pain as a result of being fired from a job I loved. Yet, I learned that I had to face it, trace it, and erase it so I could replace it. I had to Face It, face the fact that I had been fired. Then I had to Trace It, and learn from the situation. Next, I had to Erase It, erase the anger I had and not let that anger hold me back from growing to the next level. Finally, I had to Replace It, replace that negative experience with a new positive experience.

I took a job with the school system as a drug prevention coordinator. As part of my job, I started giving speeches to kids about staying away from drugs. Then I was invited to speak for teachers to help them develop a positive attitude in the midst of challenging times. I soon started to speak at churches and companies. Then I started traveling and writing books. I started hosting television and radio programs. A decade after being fired, I was named one of the "Outstanding Five Speakers in the World" by Toastmasters International and inducted into the Speakers

Hall of Fame. Pain can be a huge motivational and transformational force, which is why this book is so powerful.

In his book, Dr. Evans shares a new perspective about how you actually can become stronger when you run to the pain. He points out, so wonderfully, that when we learn to think of pain differently, we can come to the realization that pain has the capacity to become an ally rather than a feared enemy.

Dr. Evans lays out a step-by-step program to find the best of yourself through the process. I love how he shares his own pains and disappointments. He describes how he didn't just GO through the pain, but was able to GROW through it. And now, you can do the same.

Dr. Evans explains how there are different types of pain and how pain can be an educator. It can be an indication or a heads-up about a physical issue that needs to be addressed or an emotional issue that is keeping us from being all that we can be.

Dr. Evans is a popular therapist, who is noted in *Psychology Today* as a "Behavioral Health Superhero." He sees what's beneath the surface... what's behind your mask... the motivation behind your behavior. Yet, he doesn't want you to think that a few minutes with him will make everything okay and that your pain will disappear. It takes work, or as he so aptly states in his book, "The magic begins and ends with you!"

If you are willing to read this book and do the work that he has outlined in detail, you will be changed and transformed. You can become your own superhero in your own world. Dr. Evans will help you think differently, act differently, realign your expectations and outcomes, and develop new patterns of how you handle pain, anger, disappointment, and frustration.

I especially loved the section in the book on growing through adversity. He brilliantly points out how you can become a more powerful and productive person when you follow through the step-by-step process he lays out! He says that your mission (should you choose to accept it), is to go to the pain, grow through the pain, and then expand your impact because of the power that you have developed in the process.

I recommend you read this book, then re-read it and share it with your friends and family members. You will be better, they will be better, and the world will be better. The reason the world will be better is simple. If you take an apple and cut it in half, take all the seeds out, and lay them on a table, you can count the number of seeds that came from that apple. Yet, if you take those seeds and plant them, you can never count the number of apples that can come from those few seeds.

And I contend that you if you go through the program and process that Dr. Evans lays out, you will be like the proverbial Johnny Appleseed, who spread seeds and created huge apple orchards. You will read this book and be changed; and then you will share it with others and they will be changed; and their change will spread to their family and friends. In time, we will see entire communities change. In other words, people will share the positive seeds they get from this book with others and from those seeds, many trees will grow.

Run to the Pain…. so you will be able to grow through the pain and become all you were meant to be!

- **Dr. Willie Jolley**

Preface

My friend Greg Ingram once told me, "All of us parents owe our first-born children a great debt of gratitude." That's the child we make mistakes with. The child we experiment and grow with. I was twenty years old when I had my first son Shawn. At that time, I was studying psychology, human development, and social learning. I understood that we learn how to interface with the world around us by observing how others do it. So, to ensure that Shawn wasn't a punk, (my way of thinking twenty-one years ago) whenever he fell, rather than look at him with fear in my eyes, I always made sure to display an expression of elation while yelling, "HOP UP!" In turn, he would bounce off the ground like a basketball. It truly was astonishing. I cannot remember a time when he cried after a fall. In fact, he went on to climb trees and play sports such as football, where he would fervently throw his body into another kid, shoulder first, at full speed. That was when I first realized the importance of how we view pain and allow it to function in our lives.

In June of 2015, I was convinced by a few friends to join them in a "Tough Mudder Race." This event consisted of 10 miles of obstacles, including mud pits and plenty of lifting and climbing. Although I had been exercising regularly prior to the event, I was not close to being physically prepared for this race. Several times throughout the course, my body locked up with severe muscle spasms; yet, I was determined to make it through every barrier even though we had a choice to skip obstacles. By the end of the race, several hours after the start, I staggered across the finish line with legs that screamed for first aid. With assistance from my girlfriend (now wife) I made it to a hot bath and soaked for the night.

The entire evening, I thought about how I would approach my recovery. I mostly thought about the pain I was going to endure getting myself back to running. Having been an athlete my entire life, I had gone through periods of recovery when I would take a few days off after an extreme workout to give my muscles time to recover. This process was especially important if I was coming back from some time off and needed to ease myself back into a regular workout regimen.

I thought about this process and how it would usually take a couple of weeks to bounce back from an event that challenged my body so strenuously. This time, I did not want the process to take so long. My only reservation was the pain. I resolved that I would get myself into the gym on the very next day, even if it was just to walk on the treadmill. This way I could gradually get myself adjusted to the aching of my muscles. So, I did. And, not only did I walk on the treadmill, I was able to get up to a jog. As you can imagine, this was a painstaking process until my legs warmed up and I was able to stretch. The next day, I did the same thing, and this time there was a little less pain than the first day. By the end of the week, and after jogging and stretching every day, I was back to running full-speed. I was able to cut my recovery time in half. If I had waited a couple of days to get back to work, it would have surely dragged out my recovery process.

During this week of running towards the pain, I thought about other areas of my life where this process could apply. I thought about emotional pain from losing a loved one or being betrayed. I thought about the psychological pain associated with anxiety, depression, or feeling like a failure. It was then that I realized, in every aspect of our lives, physically, emotionally, and psychologically, the quickest way to heal from trauma, is to not walk, but run towards the pain.

Introduction

There are many people who feel trapped, like hamsters on a wheel, day in and day out, simply living their lives with the acceptance that they will be in constant pain. They feel physical pain from injuries they have not addressed with a doctor, or maybe they are avoiding a surgery for whatever reason. They feel pain because they have not spoken to their child, their parent, or siblings for quite some time after a falling out. They feel pain from the loss of a loved one which has not subsided. They are agonized by depression or anxiety, partly because they have avoided the appropriate psychological and/or psychotropic treatments. I know, because I was one of those people who buried pain and did not face it. I ran from it. So, the pain ate away at me from the inside and slowed down my growth. I found myself feeling exhausted but making little to no improvement with respect to healing from past trauma. The suppressed pain showed up in ways that did not match my character and blemished my integrity. Ignorance and fear were in the way of my healing, and I just did not know where to begin.

An example of this is when I was in a failing marriage. After years of fruitless arguments, I chose to avoid the pain in lieu of confronting it. I stopped talking. I shut off my feelings to protect them and I attempted to supplement my needs outside of my marriage. As a result of shutting off my emotions, venom bled into my passions, my interests, and my overall motivation to evolve. Eventually, I became numb. I followed the blueprint for proficiently ending a marriage and I was successful.

Running away from pain resulted in more anguish, and not just for me, but for my children, family, and friends. That lesson is why this book is so significant. It will teach you the purpose of pain and how to embrace it. It will also teach you how to use the pain to your advantage. Moreover, it will provide the straightest path to trauma recovery, which is to *run towards the pain.*

People have been socialized to correlate pain with negativity. Therefore, they naturally run away from pain and anything that could potentially lead to discomfort, such as adversity of any sort, hard work, difficult relationships, failure or the risk of failure, and places or activities that are reminders of lost loved ones. The key to trauma recovery is to realize there is no recovery without facing the very thing that has caused you suffering. This book will help you to redefine pain by disconnecting previous associations and establishing renewed neuro-connections with positive and fertile patterns of thought.

After reading this book, the feelings you previously correlated with your viewpoint of pain and past trauma will be your choice to carry. I promise, you will no longer be ignorant to the fact that you can truly heal, and you will have the steps to do it. Any fear linked to the process of facing your pain will be contested and you will again be faced with a decision to make. You may desire to remain oblivious, feel secure in your bewilderment, and content with your inertia or you will yearn to finally heal and leave your trauma behind you.

Please do not fall victim to the deception of futile *conditioning*. After years of living with the burdens of pain, guilt, and fear, you may have become comfortable in the midst of your discomfort. In essence, you may have normalized your pain so much that you will fight to stay in it rather than scrape to get out of it. It's like being in an abusive relationship so long that you have convinced yourself that you are just fine and there is no use leaving. In that case, you have effectually persuaded yourself to believe that your meager existence is the best that you can do. If this frame of mind is you, this book will give you the tools to eradicate that fallacy. It will be up to you to use them. Do not waste time! And Do Not Just Act Now, Act Right Now!

Trust me, I am leading by example when it comes to running towards the pain. In fact, to write this book, for the first time in my career I took an entire month off, simply to focus, dedicate energy, and minimize distractions. As an independent entrepreneur, one who has yet to move to the next phase of business where I can make money while I'm away from my clients, it means a loss of finances when I don't see them. In addition to that, I left my clients to practice their therapeutic strategies with minimal support for a month, which is easier said than done.

This is a trauma recovery book. It focuses on pain because pain is the most common denominator when it comes to trauma. It will also provide practical steps to *forgiveness* which is an absolute requirement to overcome trauma. In essence, in every aspect of life, one must discover the root of any pain and follow the most efficient steps to resolve it. Otherwise, the pain will impede progress in that particular area of his/her life. I am not a medical doctor, so this book will not be filled with a bunch of medical terms to define pain. It will give you fundamental concepts and practical steps that will ultimately empower you to sit in the driver's seat with respect to how you choose to interpret pain.

This book will provide evidence-based equations for how to acquire Motivation, Resiliency, Intentionality, and how to overcome Adversity. All of the steps and equations within this book have proven to be effective in private practice.

The words ***Pain, Trauma,*** and ***Adversity*** will be used interchangeably going forward. The material within this book has been informed by personal experiences, education, and training, along with over two decades of direct clinical service with hundreds of clients in multiple arenas that include hospital settings, group homes, special-education, foster-care services, community corrections, residential treatment facilities, outpatient facilities, and private practice. Client experiences will be slightly altered to protect the identity of the client.

So, without further ado, let's get started.

Chapter One

Pain

"The world breaks everyone and afterward many are strong at the broken places."

— *Ernest Hemingway*

How Do We Know Pain is Pain?

Pain is the body's alarm system. When those smoke detectors start screaming in your house, they can be very annoying; however, if they did not shriek at the appropriate moments, it could mean life or death. The same goes for our body's alarm system. Pain is not a bad thing.

Pain is an indication that work is being done or work needs to be done.

"Pain is a protective mechanism for the body. It occurs whenever any tissues are being damaged, and it causes the individual to react to remove the pain stimulus." (Guyton, 1981) It's your body's way of saying, "Hey! Pay attention to me!"

Pain is triggered by the body's central and peripheral nervous systems. The brain and spinal cord (central nervous system) work in concert with the body's sensory and motor nerves (peripheral nervous system) to send signals back and forth regarding sensations that ultimately register as pain or pleasure. This signal is how we know we are being touched by the sharp edge of a blade versus a feather. (Beazley-Long, Durrant, Swift & Donaldson, 2018; Lattanzi, Maftei, Marconi, Florenzano, Franchi, Borsani, Rodella, Balboni, Salvadori, Sacerdote & Negri, 2015)

The areas of the brain that I want to zero in on are the thalamus and the limbic system. These areas are where pain is ultimately interpreted, assigned to an emotion, and filed away for later. After the work of the central and peripheral nervous systems are done, the job is passed along to the thalamus which then assigns the task to the limbic system to attach an emotion to the experience. (Shih, Kuan & Shyu, 2017; Tamaddonfard, Erfanparast, Ghasemi, Henareh-Chareh, Hadidi, Mirzakhani, Seyedin, Taati, Salighedar, Salimi & Safaei, 2016; Wu, Wang, Stein, Aziz & Green, 2014) This is a very simplified way of explaining the science of pain, as contemporary research suggests that the process of experiencing acute and chronic pain can be extremely dense and multifaceted. (Page, 2015; Seymour & Mancini, 2020)

"Pain is always subjective. Each individual learns the application of the word through experiences related to injury in early life." (Anand, 1996; Merskey, 1991) In other words, what is noteworthy and equally exciting is that the physical process of feeling pain requires a learned association between an event and an emotion. Accordingly, we typically learn to associate the sensation of having our finger pricked with a negative emotion. Many people have already assigned certain sensations with a negative emotion. However, the good news is we have the power to rewire how we respond to events that were once painful. Cutting-edge research supports the influence of treatments such as acupuncture, meditation, and hypnosis as effective methods to mitigate physical pain. (DePascalis, Varriale & Cacace, 2015; Nakata, Sakamoto & Kakigi, 2014; Santiago, Tumilty, Macznik & Mani, 2016) Thus, with intentionality and consistent effort, we have the ability to reassign activities, behaviors of others, and various experiences that we once viewed as undesirable or negative, to a positive and even joyful feeling.

The process of reconditioning how we respond to pain is the same for physical, emotional, and psychological trauma. In each case, if we choose to avoid or bury the pain, the impact on your ability to function in all aspects of life can be catastrophic. From the loss of a limb and/or long-term physical debilitation, to an inability to establish and maintain meaningful relationships, trust issues, and many more infectious symptoms can result from a failure to ***hear your body's alarm system and simply listen, then to take action***. Consider as I demonstrate the effects of evading or suppressing physical, emotional, or psychological pain.

Running Away from Physical Pain

Have you ever had a pestering injury that kept reminding you that it was not going anywhere? When you finally got it checked out, you realized if you had just gone to have it looked at earlier, the problem would have been resolved much sooner. You probably put it off because you didn't want to spend the time to have it looked at. Well, if you moved quicker, you would have spent precious time on the front end having the injury tended to, but then your journey back to full recovery would have begun at the moment when you had the injury evaluated.

The healing process cannot begin until your injuries receive the attention they deserve and require.

What happens if we choose to ignore our body's alarm system? Just as ignoring a smoke alarm in your house can lead to property damage or death, so can ignoring your body's way of telling you to pay attention. Get in the habit of scheduling regular check-ups, and if your body speaks to you, *simply listen, then take action*. If you do not tend to an open wound, it will get infected. Infection occurs when a microorganism enters the body, and this is more likely to happen while the body's defenses are down.

When we do not run towards our physical pain, it weakens our defense system.

Once acute pain becomes chronic due to inattentiveness, it is safe to say that long-lasting detrimental effects can ensue. In life, either we choose to ignore nagging injuries, tolerating them in our daily lives or we choose to face the pain unflinchingly and resolve the injury straightaway.

> *Sometimes it requires a surgical procedure or a professional to intervene and assist with a proper and speedy recovery.*

In 1998, I was in undergraduate school playing football and suffered a devastating knee injury. I underwent a reconstructive knee surgery and while in the hospital recovery bed, I remember being placed on a morphine drip. All I had to do was press a button and the pain would subside. After hitting that button, I knew it was a dangerous substance, because it eliminated my pain so quickly. After pressing the button once or twice, I was afraid to hit it again, so I didn't. I remember feeling the agonizing pain of the heavy cast as it pulled on freshly sutured wounds while I staggered to the bathroom. Yet, I had been exposed to drug addicts my entire life due to my mother's field of work as an Addictions Counselor, so I was very familiar with the effects of heroin and some prescription pain medications.

Thus, I had a very negative perception of narcotics. When I was released, I was prescribed codeine-based medications to help me tolerate the pain. I remember taking a dose of the medication and actually feeling the pain get sucked from my leg. That was the last time I took that medication. Unbeknown to me, the decision to tolerate the pain and refrain from taking those medications would forever frame my view of pain management.

The 5-Second Rule

I did not know it then, but in hindsight I was conditioning myself to handle pain in a particular way. I was teaching myself to avoid relying on a crutch when it came to self-healing. I was also conditioning myself to face pain head-on. I just wish I really knew the power of what I was doing and how that power could transcend physical pain to emotional and psychological trauma as well.

Have you ever heard of *"The 5-Second Rule?"* This is the "universal law," at least that's what we told ourselves as children, that if some food hits the ground, provided it does not fall in something reprehensible such as an unknown liquid or substance, you are free to pick it up and eat it as long as it's done within a 5-second window. Now, this law may be germane to a specific group, era, socio-economic class, or subculture. Who knows? I just know it applied to me. And even today, depending on where I am and if someone is looking, the rule may still apply. When it comes to physical pain, I currently practice the same principle of the "5-Second Rule."

Because I am cognizant of self-conditioning, I have been careful to avoid allowing myself to languish in pain when something happens. I give myself no more than five seconds for the pain to hit me, for me to feel it and then release it. This is a strategy I have been practicing for years, so it may take some time for you to implement it. As an athlete who played football, basketball, and ran track, it is understood that pain tolerance is essential to individual and collective success in competition. It is drummed into the minds of young athletes during every practice and especially during the games. I remember chanting phrases as a team such as, "Pain is weakness leaving the body!" We were being conditioned to tolerate pain and move its physical effects into a space in our brain where we could manipulate it and allow the pain to work in our favor when our bodies were exhausted and we could only appeal to the inner fortitude of our minds to finish a play or make a move. Going forward, practice giving yourself a maximum of five seconds to eliminate acute physical pain.

Running Away from Emotional Pain

While in private practice, I worked with a client who lost his father in a terrible car accident. His dad had a heart attack while driving to do this client a favor and the accident was fatal. He lost his father many years prior to therapy, yet the grief continued to haunt him. As a way to cope with the loss, he assigned a negative emotion to all of the previously enjoyable activities that he and his father shared together. Consequently, he stopped doing activities such as bowling and Father's Day activities. These were previously significant influences on his happiness which he no longer experienced. The avoidance of places, holidays, and events impeded the growth of significant relationships in his life. It also restricted his joy and stunted his skill development in activities where he was naturally gifted and that he loved. During therapy, to heal from the trauma of losing his father, he needed to not only face the event and forgive both himself and his father, he also needed to begin to re-associate the once enjoyable activities he loved with positive emotions. To heal from the pain, he had to dig up the things he buried away for so long and learn to embrace them.

It does not hurt to allow for some things to continue to be assigned to a negative emotion. Some things are simply not good. My client may never be happy when thinking about the loss of his dad. However, it becomes problematic when we allow ourselves to hold onto the initial negative emotion that we once felt and give that emotion permission to navigate our lives and bleed into our daily activities. We must learn to let it go. My client cannot allow himself to live in turmoil for the rest of his life due to the loss he sustained, especially if the feeling is going to impede progress in his life.

How do you allow emotional pain to operate in your life? A friend, Christy Johnson, lost her daughter who was the victim of a tragic domestic-violence relationship. Her daughter, Destiny, was murdered. The perpetrator was not convicted of her murder, although Christy knew in her gut what happened to her daughter and by whom. Christy faced her emotional pain directly. She began a non-profit organization named Finding Your Destiny. Her organization is dedicated to saving and supporting victims of domestic-violence relationships. Christy chose to allow her emotional pain to become fuel.

We will all encounter emotional pain in the form of grief and loss and it is in that moment, we can choose to use the pain as fuel or added weight for our life's journey.

Just as ignoring physical pain can lead to infection of our blood, **ignoring emotional pain can lead to infection of our heart**. Infection of the heart is exhibited but not limited to the following symptoms:

- Broken and *unresolved relationships*
- Power and *control issues*
- Lack of ability to build or sustain *trust* within relationships
- Lack of *passion for life*
- Lack of interest in *pursuing dreams*

- Lack of interest in *developing gifts and talents*
- Lack of ability to effectively *regulate emotions*
- Lack of *self-fulfillment*
- Lack of *self-efficacy*
- Lack of *self-esteem*
- Lack of ability to be *vulnerable*
- Lack of ability and/or desire to *love*
- Lack of desire to *build a family*
- Lack of desire to be in a *monogamous relationship*

The 5-Star Process

There are different levels of trauma and some experiences are so severe that the body will respond in ways that will protect you from the impact of the event. You could go into shock, in which case, you may become completely numb of emotions and feelings of any kind. *The 5-Star Process* is a strategy that can only be used if you are completely present emotionally after the event. For example, if you fail an exam or lose someone you love or suffer a loss that is tolerable, then these steps may be helpful in establishing a process for quickly overcoming a negatively impactful event.

Step #1 Allow yourself to release. For various reasons, people associate crying and tears with weakness or emotions with being soft. For some people, there is no outlet for emotional anguish, so they stuff the pain deep inside. Allow yourself to be fully present in the moment and release all of what you are feeling. If you need to scream out loud, cry, curse, run some miles, hit the heavy bag, write in your journal, or just hold someone you love, then allow yourself the freedom of self-expression. I don't believe in becoming violent or destructive when upset, so this is not permission to do anything that will harm you or someone else or destroy any property. Additionally, unless you are venting to a person who is volunteering his/her time, do not force your emotions on anyone else. If you are upset because your partner is breaking up with you, do not spend time attempting to unload your emotional baggage on that person. That's a quick way to earn yourself a civil protection order. Release your emotions either in private or amongst those who welcome your struggle and wish to help you. A professional is always an acceptable option.

There is a time limit on this process. Again, for severe matters associated with grief and loss, you may need some additional time, so do not vilify yourself if you need more time than you expected to get your emotions out. The key is to establish a reasonable time when you will snap out of the funk and be intentional about moving forward with your life. You must condition yourself to process your feelings in a healthy manner that will not leave your daily responsibilities deprived. I suggest starting off with an aim for no more than 24 hours of freedom to release your emotions.

Step #2 Identify where to direct your emotions. People oftentimes displace their emotional pain and blame everyone other than themselves. They will curse God. They will curse their friends or anyone connected to the traumatic event, when the reality is that oftentimes the true culprit is one's self. In these cases, the person suffering will need to forgive him/herself for the role played in the pain he/she is suffering.

People find themselves wanting to control the consequences for their actions. That level of control is frequently outside of our reach. *Understand that the decisions you make will impact the rest of your life, and you cannot always predict the results.* If you make a decision and the ending does not turn out the way you would have wanted, do not be infuriated with anyone other than you. I work with people who have major rage issues, and often times they are angry because they cannot control the outcome of a situation. Accordingly, they choose to be angry at the person or the situation they cannot manipulate. In these instances, their anger is displaced and their emotions should be redirected towards themselves.

Step #3 Accept what can and cannot be changed.
You have taken a day to release your emotions and you have identified who or what contributed to your emotional distress. Now you need to acknowledge whether or not there is anything you can do to improve the situation. If there is, think through your approach to executing the changes and make them happen. If you discover there is nothing that can be done, permit that fact to sink in.

Embrace it and move on to the lessons learned from the experience.

Step #4 Record lessons learned. Evaluate the situation and identify your role. Record the lessons learned and what should be improved in the case of future occurrences. The most significant facet of a traumatic event is the life lessons left in the rubble. Do not squander a noteworthy loss by failing to file away the teaching moments. Set the appropriate tone for how to handle the same misfortune in the future, for similar events will undoubtedly replicate themselves again. Ways of recording this process could range from journaling to audio recording. Either way, documentation is crucial because you can always refer back to your method of recording the lessons learned. In essence, ensure that you are paying meticulous attention to every experience that causes you to feel emotional distress.

Step #5 Continue with daily activities. Guarantee that you continue to take care of yourself. Note your appetite, your sleeping patterns, your desire to get up and go, your motivation to take care of yourself with a daily hygiene regimen, or any shift in your typical daily activities. If people close to you are bringing these types of concerns to your attention, allow them to do so. They may recognize something that you don't see. Depression is something that touches us all at some point in our lives and on various levels. The key is to not allow our emotions to draw us down into an abyss that we cannot escape. Also, do not be afraid of seeking professional assistance when processing any level of grief. There is absolutely nothing wrong with additional support along this voyage we call life.

Running Away from Psychological Pain

One of the principle dangers of suppressing psychological pain is that people can fool themselves into believing everything is fine and that there is no need to be concerned with their psychological health. The risk involved with this is that

We are always conditioning ourselves.

And we can inadvertently condition ourselves to be comfortable in an unhealthy and maladaptive state.

One of my clients living with Attention Deficit Hyperactivity Disorder and Generalized Anxiety Disorder had been managing her symptoms for quite some time with minimal assistance. She is married with children and fortunately she was able to channel many of the symptoms influenced by her psychological health into behaviors that benefited her family. She would cook, clean, and grocery shop compulsively. Although she loved to do those activities and she was gifted in those areas, they completely consumed her and she desired assistance from her husband and more personal time for herself. Alas, her inattention to her trials with excessive worrying, disorganization, self-care, impulsiveness, hyperactivity, and focus created a reality for her, her marriage, and her family that ultimately equaled up to discontent spiraling into depression.

It was not until she unpacked all of the distorted thoughts and misappropriated coping strategies incubating her suffocating way of living, that she tasted true liberation and self-actualization. To treat her psychological wounds, it was necessary for us to dive into her honest perspective and acceptance of herself, as well as to assist her with developing her vision of her best self-representation. This is the work that too often people shy away from when it comes to therapy. The effort to evaluate and discover the sincerest essence of self, is what therapy is all about, and for some people, they would rather walk through life not knowing who they really are. For them, finding out who they are is terrifying, because deep down, they do not believe they will like what they discover.

Who you have always been, does not have to remain who you will always be!

Ignorance

Ignorance, disinformation, and fear often hinder people from pursuing the necessary treatment to address their psychological pain. In some cases, you don't know what you don't know. For these people, they may be uncomfortable with their existence, but do not know where to put their finger on their issue. They have no idea that talking about their feelings could help because for them, their situation is their normal.

If you are reading this book, and you feel a sense of perplexity with life, start with simply talking about your thoughts and feelings. Be careful with who you talk to and the information you receive. You may not always have immediate access to the most appropriate resources, but you have to start somewhere. Just know, all counsel is not wise counsel. If your resource is not encouraging you to continue with self- exploration, they may be trapped just as you are, thus providing you with information that will keep you mystified. In today's times, many cities are very progressive with respect to mental health, and they provide free local hotlines available for people to call and ask questions or simply talk. You may need to start there.

Just Start!

Disinformation

Are you the type of person who will not go see a movie based on someone else's experience? Will you avoid tasting food because someone else did not like it? Do you allow another person's failures or dissatisfaction with life's offerings to influence your attempts to merely try? If so, you may easily fall prey to *disinformation*. Two people can go to the same school. One of them may graduate, apply the knowledge gained, and become a millionaire, while the other person graduates, does absolutely nothing with the knowledge garnered, and becomes homeless. At the end of the day, change boils down to the individual. With this in mind, do not allow anyone to dissuade you from pursuing therapy or help of any kind when you are on a quest for self-discovery and self-improvement.

Some people go to therapy and have a terrible experience because their expectation is that the therapist will sprinkle some magic dust on their head, and they will be miraculously absolved of all past trauma, emotional deregulation, mental anguish, anxiety and heartache. Just so you know, that is a completely false narrative.

The magic begins and ends with you!

A therapist is purely a tour guide walking with you side-by-side through your journey and offering various perspectives and insights that may help you as you decide which way you want to go. They also help you to unpack the weighty and crippling luggage you may have packed while replacing it with light and aerodynamic luggage that will make your journey as gratifying as possible. Moreover, a therapist is a splendid addition to anyone's life journey. If you had a choice, why pass up on a tour guide?

Fear

Fear is the number one motivator in existence. Similar to pain, we have the power to determine how we allow fear to function in our lives. It can either keep you frozen in suspension, or it can provide the necessary fire for you to seek change. ***How is fear operating in your life?***

- Fear of *The Unknown*
- Fear of *Discomfort*
- Fear of *Failure*
- Fear of *Embarrassment*
- Fear of *Losing Friendships or Support*
- Fear of *Rejection*
- Fear of *Heartbreak*

The fact is, we must be willing to experience all of the above to develop resilience, and resiliency is essential to overcoming adversity.

Once you experience failure the first time, your skin becomes a little more tough in preparation for future failures.

Are you living or are you merely surviving? I often ask my clients, "Would you rather experience the best possible feeling only to lose it after a short while, or never experience that feeling at all?" What is most ironic is that many individuals are afraid of trying something new due to fear of experiencing discomfort, even when they are seemingly desperate to get out of their current state of discomfort. At that point, what do you have to lose?

Chapter 2
Conditioning

"You just can't let life happen to you; you have to make life happen."

— *Idowu Koyenikan*

As you go through life experiencing pain, remember that we are always *conditioning* ourselves. Be mindful of how you manage physical, emotional, and psychological pain. We can condition ourselves to handle situations poorly simply by making insufficient practices our routine. The trick is to take control of your condition. To do this, you must become intentional. *Intentionality* was the word of focus for all of the year 2019. This word saved and changed lives by way of the following equation:

$$\textit{Self-Awareness + Desire = Intentionality}$$

Self-Awareness

If you make it a practice of slamming things, yelling and cursing, or becoming violent when you are angry, remember that you have been conditioning yourself to respond this way when you are upset. If you handle grief by drinking away your sorrows, isolating yourself from others, and refusing to participate in pro-social activities, you are preparing yourself to handle the next loss in the same exact fashion. If you recover from failure by quitting, refusing to try again, or declining new opportunities, at best, you can look forward to remaining exactly where you currently stand in life. The cold and hard truth is that you do not have to settle for this behavior. You do not have to accept an unfitting version of yourself. If your behavior is not the best illustration of who you would like to be, your first step is to become *Self Aware*. Recognize the behavior that you would like to change along with all of the factors influencing your behavior. Identify the contributing factors to who you are! The factors you identify will come in handy later in this text.

Desire

Once you are aware of who you have been, you must identify who you would like to be. What is your *Desire*? It is not enough to know that you have been behaving in an unbecoming manner. There are plenty of people who brashly accept the fact that they are Jerks. They even wear it like a badge of honor. Your mission, should you choose to accept it, is to determine if you desire to reject your previous self and become a better representation of you. Don't lose yourself in the falsehood that *you are who you are*, as if you do not possess the power of change. Yes, you have been who you have been. Nevertheless, each day we are presented with an opportunity to do it better than we did it before. As I explain to my clients, each day we should wake up a different person from who we were the day before.

Intentionality

Now that you have become self-aware, you *know better*. And, since you have a desire to *do better*, the final step to compel yourself is to be *Intentional*. This means, despite the factors influencing who you have been, you must make a concerted effort to implement behaviors that will move you closer to that which you desire. Two things block the path to intentionality: *Emotions* and *Distorted Thinking*.

Emotions

I ran into a friend at the gym one day and he told me that he had good news. He discovered that he was cancer free. He had a scare when he went to obtain a physical and being over 40 years old, he had his prostate checked. During the process of having tests run, he did not tell his wife of his concerns. He wanted to find out if there was anything to worry about before telling her. On the day I saw him in the gym, he was planning to take her to lunch and explain everything to her, including the good news. While in the gym, he received a phone call from her that upset him. After the conversation, he was completely thrown off. "I'm not taking her to lunch, and I'm not telling her anything!" he exclaimed. His emotions completely consumed him and were blinding him of his desire to inform her of his health scare.

These are the moments where intentionality counts the most! It is not when the day is going perfect and there are no worries. Conversely, the moment we feel the gut-punch of being insulted or while feeling unappreciated or even humiliated, we must keep our eye on our genuine desire and press forward. I asked my friend, "How did the conversation you had with your wife change your desire to include her in your healthcare needs and concerns?" The reality was, although he was feeling upset for the moment, his desire to have this crucially important conversation with his wife remained the same. Therefore, he needed to set his emotions aside for that moment and still follow through with taking his wife to lunch and having the conversation.

    My friend is not alone. Every day we are presented with reasons, legitimate and frivolous, to falter on our intentions to complete tasks. These tasks can be for others as well as ourselves. It does not matter who the beneficiary of your efforts is, what is constant is that you must remain faithful to your ultimate desire, notwithstanding any emotions that may get in the way. A strategy I use to assist me with remaining intentional while feeling irritated is to keep in mind that I am always conditioning myself. Because my goal is to be a person who is able to move with intention to complete my goals even when I do not feel like it, I practice doing positive things when I am upset. An example is stopping to pick up flowers on the way home for my wife after she did something that irritated me. I am still working to improve this area for myself; however, my desire is clear, and it is up to me to remain intentional so that it becomes second nature.

Distorted Thinking

Our dreams, future, success, happiness, desires, fears, limitations, past trauma, worries, pain, pleasures, and our very existence all live in our thoughts, which are housed in our minds. We have the power to bring life or destruction to anything we attempt, simply by thinking it into existence. Anybody who is a boxing fan and was around during the Mike Tyson era knows that most of Tyson's fights were won before he even stepped foot into the ring. There were opponents who almost ran to the ground after just a swing from Tyson. I would argue that they defeated themselves with distorted thinking before they were hit with one punch.

We are simultaneously our biggest ally and adversary when it comes to progress. Pertaining to change, we will talk ourselves out of doing something new, just so that we can remain comfortable. What's crazy is we can be tormented in an extremely uncomfortable situation, and when presented with an opportunity to change the circumstances, we will attempt to talk ourselves out of making a move. In some cases, our minds and bodies become so accustomed to being in an uncomfortable state, when we have a chance to be free, we will recreate that very stifling condition. One of my friends was locked up for about ten years of his life. During that time, he experienced trauma and survived within a hostile environment that compulsorily required him to move both defensively and offensively. He has been out of prison now for sixteen years and still has trouble sleeping through the night in a comfortable bed. By his account, sometimes he ends up finishing the night on the floor.

There is a two-step process to dominating distorted thinking. We must commit ourselves physically to realign ourselves mentally. Realignment can be challenging in the beginning. Anything that has been sedentary in a position over time will give you some trouble when it's time to maneuver it. If we reposition a chair after a day on carpet, it will leave an imprint in the floor. This imprint especially goes for our understanding. The mind can be an arduous thing to change. It's funny how our brains are so intuitive when it comes to comfort. This is because every moment, our brain is attempting to preserve energy. It's almost as if we have a built-in energy preservation device working to save our strength. The good news is we can train our mind and body to become accustomed to any set of circumstances. Our brain will adjust to the condition we place it in. This is both empowering and very concerning because it means we are in possession of unlimited power.

Mental Realignment. Mental realignment is a bi-product of physical repetition. Consistency wins! Your body will be on autopilot long before you can take your hands of the wheel mentally. You may feel content with the condition of your body and still struggle with your thoughts. This process surely reverberated for me at the beginning of year 2020. We were faced with the COVID-19 pandemic, which devastated the world. The United States surpassed China and other countries around the world to become the frontrunner for the disease, leading the world in infections and deaths. On March 5th, 2020, the governor of Maryland Larry Hogan, declared a state of emergency, and by March 23rd, 2020, all non-essential businesses in Maryland, where I live, were shut down. This meant that my usual options for exercise were non-existent. At that point, I was faced with the same decision as most people around the world who were required to quarantine. Either use the quarantine as an opportunity to catch up on rest and allow myself to become lazy or find a way to 'get 'er done!'

Behavioral conditioning dictates that every position we put ourselves in is preparing us for the next move. Since this was the first global pandemic that I experienced, my thought was, "Whatever I choose to do at this moment will set the tone for how I may handle future pandemics or similar situations." So, not only did I decide to exercise the three to four days weekly that I was doing prior to the pandemic, I decided I would exercise every day. To do this, I needed to push myself physically to realign myself mentally. I understood that my mind would kick in during the process and every step I took while running or every mile I rode while cycling would be replete with thoughts of discouragement and yearning for comfort. I knew that I needed to transition my old comfort zone to a new place of comfort. Each day, and every exercise I had to decide which me I wanted to win. The old me, or the soon to be new me.

Thought Replacement. Every day, I pushed through the thoughts telling me, "You know you don't have to do this right?!" "Go ahead and stop early!" "Why are you putting yourself through this?" "Nobody will know that you didn't finish!" It became easier to ignore and replace these thoughts with positive self-talk such as, "You got this!" "It's you versus you!" "Condition yourself to be better!" "Ignore that noise and focus on the music!" Before I knew it, my body was on autopilot and it followed through with exercises, despite the clamor of distorted thoughts. Now, although I know those thoughts will come, they are faded into the background and are insignificant. I now trust my body to follow through with what it has been conditioned to achieve.

Know that distorted thinking will show up when you are attempting to do something different. Are you starting a new business? Changing your eating habits and/or diet? Adjusting your parenting style? Finishing school? Adjusting your exercise routine? No matter what you are attempting to change in your life, you can bet thoughts will pop up that will temp you to shelve your efforts. DON'T!!!!

Take a self-inventory and ask yourself:

- How do I manage anger?
- How do I handle grief and loss?
- How do I recover from failure and rejection?

Chapter Three
Adversity

"Adversity introduces a man to himself."
— *Albert Einstein*

Maturity is measured by one's ability to embrace change and accept obstacles and challenges as opportunities for personal growth. Adversity, like pain, is a revelation to us that we have an area of our lives that needs improving. The things that are challenging for you may not be challenging for me. Likewise, the things that I find to be difficult may be stress-free for you. In other words, we do not all share the same adversity. When you face a wall, it is an indication of your shortcomings. Thus, you need to find a means greater than you to overcome it. A wall for you may be a skip for me. We all have our own walls of adversity to climb, should you choose to improve who you are.

Be mindful of your core beliefs. Many people have come to view adversity as destructive; they have assigned an adverse emotion to it, and they have also associated adversity with distress. These are all distorted ways of conditioning yourself to respond to adversity. Conversely, when you face adversity, you should be overcome with a sense of elation and excitement. Adversity should be viewed as if a cheat code to a specific aspect of life has been revealed. Videogame makers must know this formula, because when challenging levels of a game are complete, then the gamer is rewarded with a new gift (a jewel) that will make the game easier. That is exactly how the game of life works. As we overcome adversity, we discover new jewels that make our lives easier.

Waves

When my youngest son, Roman, was three years old, we went to the Six Flags America amusement park in Largo, Maryland. They have a large wave pool which generates waves for about twenty minutes before breaking for about fifteen minutes, and then here come the waves again. To my surprise, Roman wanted to go to this pool. Towards the shallow end of the pool, the waves come crashing down and the full force of the waves are felt. Roman was just the right height to feel the complete strength of the waves. The first time a wave hit him, it lifted him off his feet and he went flying backwards. I caught his arm and when he landed, to my astonishment, with laughter and jubilation Roman ran shoulder first into the next wave. This time I didn't let go of his hand, as he surely went flying. Again, he ran full steam ahead into the next wave, and this time I joined in the fun. I couldn't help myself after watching him have such a great time. We laughed and hurled our shoulders into the waves until they subsided.

As I sat in the shallow end of the pool, I thought about how very different Roman's experience would have been if he did not want to be in the pool or maybe if the wave hit him unexpectedly. I'm sure, if I were forcing him to play in the pool, when the waves hit him, he may have responded as if he were in severe pain or drowning. I could imagine him crying and cowering as the waves approached and floundering in the shallow end of the pool as if all hope was lost. "Why didn't those waves crush his spirits?" I thought.

Attitude

Attitude! Roman *completely accepted* that he was entering a wave pool, so he totally expected to get smashed.

He was looking forward to every attempt to overpower the waves as they came crashing down. He had to have known that there was no chance of him winning the *battle of the waves*. Yet, he didn't back down, and enjoyed the experience of being thrown off his feet by the waves. Still, and most importantly, he knew that the waves were not going to kill him and that after a while, he would have a chance to recuperate his faculties and energy and go at it once again. I'm sure it didn't hurt that I was in the pool with him and he knew he had protection. So, in essence, Roman knew that he was going to win the *war of the waves*, because at the end of it all, he knew he would still be standing and that he was going to go home with new memories of his adventure. How does this apply to you?

Overstand that the design of life is precisely as exemplified by the wave pool. We all go through it without fail. Things in our lives are going fine for a period, and then here come the waves of adversity. Now, go back and read the above account of the wave pool experience with Roman, and replace the word wave(s) with the word adversity. Seriously, please go read it again and switch the words. How does that resonate for you?

Just as Roman did, we must <u>accept</u> that life is a gigantic *adversity pool*. The adversity will inevitably come crashing down like waves, so what good is it to cry, cower, and flounder when they do?

Having a positive attitude during the storms of adversity helps you to manage the adversity with grace.

Realize that soon the waves of adversity will subside, and you will survive! You will have an opportunity to recuperate your faculties and go right back at it again. Know that the waves of adversity will surely come Again, and Again, and Again!

Two things to remember; 1) Appreciate your moments of rejuvenation! And be intentional about making time for yourself to recharge! 2) Moments of adversity give you an opportunity to discover the cracks in your foundation, the chinks in your armor, so that you can be better prepared and stronger when you face those waves again. Your attitude while in the adversity pool (which is your entire life), will make all the difference in how you approach adversity.

Faith

The other thing that Roman exhibited, and that works for me and countless others, is *Faith*. Not only did he have faith in himself, but he had even more faith in his father. He knew without a shadow of a doubt that I was there to catch him when those waves lifted him off his feet. There have been times when he would leap from the top of my staircase at home into my arms with full confidence that he was not going to touch the ground. That is a steadfast faith in a power greater than his own. If you have never completely submitted to a force outside of yourself and left the final outcome up to pure trust, you may not be able to relate to this. Sometimes, that trust is not until you experience something that you can truly identify with it. When it comes to knowing with sheer absolution that you are going to survive through anything that life throws your way, you need to have faith in yourself. But regardless of whether you have faith in yourself, faith in a higher power can provide the security you need to fearlessly dive into the adversity pool of life. If you have yet to become acquainted with faith, my advice is to spend time seeking a source that is able to provide the energy that you have been unable to self-generate. To do this, you will need to practice meditation, which will give you an opportunity to listen and receive.

The most grueling facet of my doctoral program was the points during my dissertation, when I needed to seek and await approvals to move forward with my research. I was working for the federal government in community corrections and I requested to use community corrections officers as participants. This request required layers of approval. I was also required to acquire the endorsement of the agency's research and evaluation department. After waves upon waves of adversity, I reached a point where there was a brick wall before me. The department director no longer wanted to move forward with my research, and sans his blessing, I would essentially forfeit thousands of dollars and years of time and energy invested in my progression. The approval process was designed in a way that I had no other options, except to gain the support of this associate director. It was a pivotal moment in my life, my career and my education. It was a breaking point that could have snapped the back of anyone with less resiliency and fortitude.

At that moment in history, there were many unknowns. However, the one thing I did know was that I was not going to surrender my efforts, my desires, or my purpose. I did not choose to become disrespectful, belligerent, or unprofessional in any fashion. I simply pressed forward with faith and 100% self-assurance that I would overcome this wave of adversity. And I did. The solution was honestly a moment when pieces were moved on my behalf and I did not even have to lift a finger. There are moments in our lives that we can chalk up to pure luck, coincidence or metaphysical. I believe this moment to be one where a supernatural force bent the will of the universe in my favor. This was one of many points in my life when God intervened. How strong is your faith? Don't answer that too quickly, because the follow up question is, are you exercising it?

Chapter Four
Reconditioning

"I want to live my life in such a way that when I get out of bed in the morning, the devil says, 'Aw shit, he's up!'"

— *Steve Maraboli*

Don't forget:

We are always conditioning and/or reconditioning ourselves.

As the waves of life hit us, we are preparing ourselves for how to handle the next wave based on how we took on the preceding wave. I want to drum that into your psyche, because the more you keep that belief in mind, the more you will be keen with respect to how you respond to adversity. Managing grief and loss is a big one when it comes to being mindful of our conditioning.

I treated a whole immediate family in therapy after the tragic loss of their teenage daughter and sister. Initially, the parents were emotionally numb, so processing emotions with respect to special events was a challenge because they did not regain feeling for roughly a year. However, we worked on conditioning and reconditioning. How did they handle previous significant losses? Were they healthy processes or behaviors that needed reconditioning? What was safe and productive to do while grieving this loss that would promote healing and also prepare them for future (inevitable) losses?

We all held hands through the learning process, and they were able to develop healthy grieving processes that allowed them to continue functioning and healing, while preventing them from drifting into a depression. They were required to record their learned strategies, so that in the future, they can refer to their "best grieving practices" for assistance with healing. Let's ensure that we process grief in the most appropriate manner, because you will surely have an opportunity to exercise best practices. In life, we do not simply experience one or two losses. Life hits us with waves of calamity.

Adversity's Role

When we truly embrace the role of adversity in our lives, we will run towards it.

The role of adversity is to reveal our purpose.

One of the most commonly asked questions since the beginning of time is, "What is my purpose?" As I answer this question, it should feel good to know that we all share the same purpose in life. It's a two-part answer:

Each of us is purposed with discovering the best version of ourselves via the successful encountering and mastery of adversity through the use of our gifts and talents. And we are to assist others along their journey towards self-enlightenment.

We know this because of the blessing of adversity, along with our better-than-amazing physical design.

The Blessing of Adversity

Through every phase of our lives, we encounter levels of obstacles that we have the option to effectively surmount or avoid. They are unconditionally woven into the fabric of our lives and there are only ever two options to deal with them: Travel towards those obstacles or away from them. Obstacles are a breakthrough as they give us insight about ourselves that we would not have had if not for the moment we were facing a new barrier. Hence, because adversity is active in everyone's life, with no exceptions, and it actually helps us to become better versions of ourselves, its purpose must be directly linked to our life's mission. If you have been met with challenges that you chose not to face, those are areas of your life that are found wanting. By circumventing them, you are blocking your blessing and stunting your personal growth. Please do not duck your purpose.

    Another blessing of adversity is that it permits us to discover our specialized gifts and talents. Each of us is born with unique abilities that exemplify the best portrait of who we are and will also make us marketable if we choose to use them. They show up when we have a wall to climb, an impromptu speech to give, when we are suddenly attacked or cut off in traffic, when we have to make a quick decision, when it's three seconds left and we have the ball, when we haven't studied and the test is tomorrow, or that twenty-page paper is due in a couple of hours. Sometimes we bring adversity on ourselves by being careless or unprepared, but other times, we have to make a split decision and take action and that is when your gifts peek through the blinds. Pay attention to those moments. Don't ignore people when they tell you, "You are the only person I can talk to about this!" or, "You are the best at that!" You may not see the gift, but others will let you know. Believe them and clinch the gift, become familiar with it and expound upon it with great vigor. Not only is it your voucher to overcome the adversities of your life, but it can also be your meal ticket if you allow it to work for you.

Better than Amazingly Designed

Take a look at nature. All living organisms have unique instincts and possess physical attributes that provide protection and a means to eat and ultimately survive. We can go down a list of physical characteristics of wildlife that have specific purposes such as abundant speed, sharp teeth, thick skins and manes, incredible strength, camouflage skin, gills, scales, and tough shells. Some bugs look exactly like sticks or twigs on a tree. Some animals can breathe on land and under water. And here we are! Humans! At the top of the food chain. Not because of strength and speed, but because of our ability to outthink all other animals. Now, what special physical attributes do we possess that could give us an indication of our overall purpose?

Remember, everything that is living has purpose. We are all connected through the circle of life! We learned that from *The Lion King,* remember? If everything down to the smallest insect serves a purpose and their purpose is driven by what they are designed to do, then the same must go for us! We have a purpose which is driven by our design and what we are here to do. Hence the link between our journey of self-evolution and our better-than-amazing design.

We were strategically born with five senses. Touch, Sight, Hearing, Smell, and Taste. We were given so many senses so that if we lose one or two, we can still survive. Not only do these faculties assist us when it comes to survival, but they also allow us to connect with each other. Connecting with one another is the most important use of our senses. We are reminded of this by the original design of reproduction, which is for a man and woman to come together to create life. Men and women are physically crafted to fit together like a puzzle. Per the original design, there is no procreation without connection and humanity will cease to exist without furthering life.

What does all of this mean? We were not designed to do life alone or in a silo. It is intended for us to do life together, using our senses, discovering our gifts and talents, and conquering adversity with unified effort. That intention would be the truly human thing to do. If you recall, we are most human when we are using our brain to think creatively and to make life easier for ourselves. Accordingly, life is that much easier when we are taking it on together and not as individuals. As the great Caesar from *Rise of the Planet of the Apes* once said, "Apes alone weak. Apes together strong."

Back to the purpose of life. Our purpose is collective. We are to understand the role of adversity to assist us with self-discovery and growth, consistently capitalize on what we learn by continuing to reinvent ourselves with a better replica, and maximize our gifts and talents along the way, all while helping others to do the same.

Chapter Five
Learning Lessons

"Short cuts make long delays."
— *J.R.R. Tolkien*

The crucial role of adversity is to teach. When we face adversity and fail to learn, we have wasted a golden opportunity and one of our life's jewels. Sometimes we have an opportunity to learn the same lesson because we repeat the same maladaptive behaviors which lead to our initial challenges. You will know you have matured when you no longer have to face the same obstacles while experiencing the same level of difficulty.

Humility + Motivation + Resiliency = Defeat of Adversity

Humility

To face and conquer adversity, an unmatched ingredient in our change recipe is *Humility*. One of my young clients was studying for the Armed Services Vocational Aptitude Battery (ASVAB) test to enter the Navy. The first time he took it, he was ill-prepared. The test is comprised of nine sections and he only focused his efforts on studying one or two. After reviewing the results from the first failed effort, we concluded that if he concentrated his efforts towards a couple of the other areas, he could easily pass the test. He also needed to tweak a few things about how he studied the material. He learned from the first experience and adjusted his efforts prior to taking the test a second time. His efforts paid off and he passed. He did not give his pride permission to impede his ability to receive guidance or to advance.

Anxiety is something that challenges many of my clients. In my private practice, I am very clear that the most important work happens outside of therapy. The work that is done on a daily basis to implement the strategies processed in therapy is where the rubber meets the road. That work prepares them for when a panic attack or intense anxiety occurs. One of my previous clients who was extremely cynical regarding therapy and the strategies discussed, failed to implement or practice any of the strategies identified. So, when she faced moments of severe anxiety, she did not experience anything new. She continued with her same daily conditioning and practices with an expectation that things would change. She did not seize life's jewels and unfortunately continued to struggle with general anxiety and panic attacks. Contrariwise, many clients have at least attempted the strategies processed in treatment and have witnessed remarkable results.

Humility is not always easily attained. Some people are gifted with it and others require life to teach it to them. Hopefully, when life is teaching you a lesson, you will be open to receive it. Either way, to gracefully manage the adversity that life will deal you, humility is essential.

Motivation

Motivation truly boils down to one's desire to change. For some folks, it is challenging for them to see themselves beyond their current circumstances, so they don't even know that they should desire a change. For them, the first step is to realize and accept that they are *Uncomfortable*. Discomfort is at the emergence of any change process. Otherwise, why would you change? Discomfort is the stream that flows into *Vision*. Once you have accepted that your current situation is not the best representation of yourself, you will seek more. Vision is acquired by nothing less than simply pivoting your current position to acquire an alternative viewpoint. Simply seek. When you are uncomfortable and have acquired an improved vision of yourself, you are at the genesis of *Motivation.* Motivation is at the intersection of discomfort and vision.

Discomfort + Vision = Motivation

Resiliency

Resiliency is my favorite word in the dictionary. It is the one ingredient that if people can touch it, nurture it, harness the power from it, and use it as gasoline, resiliency can answer all of their dreams. Throughout my career, resiliency has proven to be the deciding factor with respect to the speed of one's recovery from any adverse situation. It is the secret to success and the difference between winning and losing. It is surely the lifeblood of innovation, engineering, and modernization. The list of inventions that required individuals and groups of people to relentlessly pursue a goal while throwing their shoulders into the waves of adversity until the job was complete is abounding: the carbon-filament light bulb invented by Lewis Latimer, the gas mask and traffic signal created by Garrett Morgan, the multiplex telegraph developed by Granville T. Woods, potato chips created by George Crum, the pacemaker invented by Otis Boykin, the lawn mower designed by John Albert Burr, touch-tone telephones developed by Dr. Shirley Ann Jackson, and the gas heating furnace invented by Alice H. Parker. The list could go on and on.

Any race of people who suffered through slavery, holocaust, or genocide of any kind, and is still thriving today was able to survive due to resiliency. Any descendent of American Chattel Slavery has the blood of resiliency coursing through your veins and surging in your heart every second! You possess the same blood of a people who were under the complete control of another race. Within your blood is the absolute power to overcome anything that could possibly be thrown at you! Africans who were Americanized were stripped from their families, beaten, whipped, tortured, brutally mutilated, killed, and dominated for almost FOUR HUNDRED years. The residual effects of hundreds of years of slavery are extensive and pervasive. Slaves were not allowed to educate themselves; they were legally considered to be less than human and every effort possible was dedicated to keeping them under the same conditions for as long as possible. If you are a descendent of people who suffered through these conditions and you are reading this, you are the recipient of a blessing. The blessing of your forefathers and mothers who led by pure vision, faith, and resiliency, who scraped and fought for you and me to be in the position we sit in today.

Resiliency is the, "I can't stop and won't stop" factor! Some people fail to realize the strength they embody sheerly by being alive. To be here, you… yes, YOU… had to beat out as many as 200 million other sperm to acquire life. So, as you can clearly see, resiliency is the attribute that should be most sought after. It is in your reach, but there is only one caveat. Ready?

The only path to Resiliency is Failure.

Failure has earned a bad reputation and does not receive the honor it deserves. Sans failure, one cannot develop resiliency. Therefore, you must attempt to change your circumstances, fail, and then attempt again to develop resiliency. There is no other path. As previously discussed, fear may be in the way of you putting one foot in front of the other. I say, take a look at your current circumstances and ask yourself if there is anything you would like to change, but you have not made a move because you are afraid. Then ask yourself how uncomfortable you are with that situation. You do not have to wait until you are unbearably uncomfortable before you decide to take action. If you are already unhappy with your situation, what difference does it make if you try to improve and you fail the first time? You have already tasted discomfort. So, whether you do something different or not, you will still be unhappy and uncomfortable!

I do suggest moving smartly when embarking on your change voyage. Here are a few tips for travel:

1. Write down your vision with a plan of attack.
2. Research your plan by observing others who have already done what you plan to do and if at all possible, talk to those people.
3. Do not quit one money maker before securing another one.

4. If you are working for someone else, build your brand while you are supporting theirs.
5. Remember, a spirit of service will advance you much sooner than a spirit of self-absorption.

Attempt
+ Failure
+ Repeated Attempts
(with Adjustments)
= Resiliency

Chapter Six
Running Towards the Pain

"Your sacred space is where you can find yourself over and over again."

— *Joseph Campbell*

Processing Pain in a Healthy Way

True enlightenment is understanding that an inherent duty embedded within our purpose, is to remain open to assistance from others.

I am a strong advocate for psychotherapy. For many people, if they have not received any support while grieving a loss, (*loss* is synonymous with any form of trauma) they will process the injury to the best of their ability. In practice, I have worked with people grieving and have witnessed them managing hurt via the manifestation of various *stages of grief*. In 1969, Elizabeth Kübler-Ross wrote in her book, *On Death and Dying,* five stages of grief that are now referred to as the Kübler-Ross model. These five stages include Denial, Anger, Bargaining, Depression, and Acceptance. Kübler-Ross laid a foundation that has been expounded upon to this day. Rightfully so, as people with little to no support often find themselves stuck in one of these stages, struggling to find healthy ways to progress and heal. Consequently, they submerge their pain deep into their subconscious mind.

The illusion of concealing the pain gives people a false confidence that they are somehow cured. They do not have to experience the emotional tension of the pain on a regular basis, so they forget about it. Until, they are reminded of it. Then they realize the heartbreaking truth that they have not healed after all. If a person who has successfully concealed any form of pain were to explore that pain with a professional, to their surprise, they would likely discover that the pain has in fact been operating in their lives in meaningful and likely unfruitful ways.

If you have not experienced psychotherapy before, I would recommend it simply to receive assistance with an exploratory journey into your life. Some people have lived through various traumas, and because they feel fine, they do not know how those traumas are influencing their daily decisions, behaviors, and relationships. Many of the clients I serve are very well-adjusted, professional, and thriving people who understand the value of two perspectives being better than one. Because they embrace this aspect of purpose, they are able to discover correlations between past traumas and current behaviors which empower them with the choice to improve their lives or remain the same.

The Secret Ingredient to Healing from Pain (Quickly)

Many people do not realize what is going on in the background when they are holding on to past hurt. You know you have not completely healed from trauma when things are seemingly going fine in your life until you hear a person's name, see a picture, smell a fragrance, hear a song, drive by a specific location, approach a holiday, or experience any number of triggers. Suddenly, that once pleasant day turns into a nightmare. Even though you may have successfully evaded your pain (by your standards) for an extended period of time, when you have negative energy lurking in your subconscious, it is working against you even when you do not realize it.

This process is similar to your cell phone; if you do not take the time to clear out the applications running in the background, your phone can become drained and glitchy. The same goes for the negative energy attached to past trauma, draining your spirit, your joy, your passion, your motivation, and your love as it works in the background of your subconscious mind.

Now, take a trip with me for a few ticks. Pick a traumatic experience that continues to rear its ugly head in your life. I do not want this exercise to cause you further trauma, so be careful with your selection. Trace the event back to the beginning. As you can admit, if this event is still causing you uneasiness, it is because someone needs to be forgiven. You may need to forgive yourself, to forgive someone else, or to forgive both someone else and yourself.

That's the cheat-code. The secret to quickly healing from any trauma is to run towards forgiveness. The quicker you can forgive, the quicker you can heal.

Forgiveness

Unforgiveness is at the root of all lingering effects of trauma. *Forgiveness* is the release of negative energy directed towards an event or person. How to do we forgive? This is a question that repeatedly comes up when helping my clients through this process. So, I went to the literature.

All the books I found on forgiveness discussed it from a spiritual perspective. This would only help those who believe in a higher power and the concept of forgiveness as it relates to the grace of that higher power. I believe it to be an awesome concept; however, I am a believer. I wanted to find practical steps for forgiveness that did not necessarily relate to forgiving others just as we have been forgiven by God. I did not find any. Thus, I developed the following steps that will assist you with learning to forgive.

Step #1 Understand the Purpose of Forgiveness

The first step to forgiveness is to understand the purpose. Why should we forgive in the first place? Let's first dispel the myth that forgiveness has anything to do with the perpetrator of the offense. How many of you are holding on to malice in your heart due to something that someone did to you? You don't speak to that person or deal with them on any level. However, you are still allowing your past interactions with them to dictate your emotions and even how you relate with others. You may argue with a new partner due to what that previous person did. You may hold back your love, refuse to trust, stop pursuing gainful employment, stop pursuing your dreams, or isolate from others as a result of that past relationship. The not-so-funny thing is, while you are busy encumbering your progress and your happiness, that person who everyone close to you knows you can't stand, who makes your blood boil, who ruins your day on sight, is most likely off living his/her best life. They don't have a care in the world and your disdain for them does nothing to slow down their joy.

Your ill-will wished upon other people, only causes you prolonged and unresolved grief.

By failing to forgive, you are sponsoring your self-destruction. Consider this: the number one cause of death is *Stress*. Actually, in America, it's heart disease, but if you reflect upon the risk factors associated with heart disease, such as high blood pressure, smoking, lack of physical activity, diabetes, and high cholesterol, you will see that stress is a chief contributor. Stress is nothing more than negative energy expressing itself within the railway system of your body. Hence, your ill-will, or unforgiveness, is parallel to negative energy traveling on the expressway of stress throughout your body, especially to your heart and your mind, drastically increasing your chances of encountering a heart attack or stroke.

Hopefully, you are able to accept the purpose of forgiveness, which again has nothing to do with the perpetrator, and everything to do with extending your life-force. The first step to forgiveness is simply being aware of this fact. Similar to being aware that you must eat and drink to survive; once you know this to be true, it is not something you have to think about. When you are thirsty, you drink and when you are hungry, you eat. Additionally, when you feel either of these sensations, you quench your thirst or hunger with urgency. Likewise, you are now aware that to quickly heal from trauma, you must forgive; so, when you feel pain, without any deferral, you are to make forgiveness a top priority.

Step #2 Identify Who to Forgive

Oftentimes, we are so busy allowing our emotions to consume us that we fail to properly identify who to forgive. Who is truly to blame for why you are feeling pain? This question can get tricky, so prior to rushing to anger or allowing yourself to remain there for an extended period of time, please do a careful evaluation of the incident in question. The last thing you want to do is displace your anger and hold a grudge against a person who should not even be on trial.

Two years ago, shortly after my son Shawn's 18th birthday, he made some decisions which resulted in consequences for which he was unprepared. Let me prime this story by stating, prior to this incident, Shawn had never been disrespectful to me a day in his life. He may have had this issue with others, but never with me. Also, he had always known that I possessed and still have a "zero tolerance" for disrespect.

Shawn had been told on more than one occasion not to eat or keep food in his bedroom. One day, my wife, his "bonus-mother," found some food in his trashcan and sent a pic of it to our group text-message. Along with the picture, she simply texted, "I thought we agreed not to have food in the room." After experiencing a short lapse of rational and constructive thought, Shawn responded in a way which could be easily interpreted as disrespectful. Rather than respond emotionally, I called him to discuss the matter. No answer. I then texted him with the instructions to call me back. Still, no response. Unfortunately for him, by the time he was ready to call me back a couple of hours later, he had made his bed and was going to lie in it for a while. As a consequence for his behavior, he was informed that he was no longer welcome in my home and that he would have to stay with his mother.

Forgiveness of Self. It took my son several months before he would even acknowledge his actions leading up to the consequences he faced. He chose to remain focused on everything other than his behaviors which started the entire event. After setting his pride aside, he was finally able to open his eyes to see and his ears to listen. He also needed to see through the fog of unproductive feedback he was receiving from people who only received part of the story.

It is a waste of time to be angry with the person who issues a sentence for a crime that we chose to commit.

If you fail to acknowledge the role you play in your wins and losses, you fail to learn from life's jewels which drastically slows your maturity, advancement, and healing.

Because Shawn was so busy being angry with me for his consequences, if asked to complete an exercise of forgiveness, he would have been focused on trying to forgive me. That would have been a gross misappropriation of energy because I wasn't the person who needed forgiving in the first place. He needed to recognize that it was his poor decisions and responses that were at the origin of his path, so he truly needed to address this and forgive himself.

Acknowledge. To forgive yourself, you must acknowledge the fact that you made the decision which directly resulted in an undesired outcome. Go back to the very beginning of the event to make this determination. Be careful not to accept the responsibility for someone else's decision. However, acknowledge and truly accept yours; otherwise, you may be faced with the same scenario in the future and you will take the same path again. In effect, you will be deciding to remain in a cycle of pain. The only way to break the cycle is to take a better path when faced with the same situation again. In Shawn's case, it all began with his decision to eat in his room and break the rules of the house.

Make Amends. It is imperative that you at least attempt to make amends for your behavior when endeavoring to forgive yourself. Once you have acknowledged to yourself that you were wrong, ensure that you inform the parties involved with the event that you were wrong as well. This is an essential aspect of releasing the burden of your choices. You must dump the contents of your actions at the feet of the individual(s) involved. This step is not for them. It is for you. Obviously, if you are attempting to forgive yourself, you have a conscience. To free your conscience, you must make amends. The situation with Shawn lasted for at least three months all because he did not acknowledge his wrongdoing or attempt to make amends.

Make Corrections. If you truly want to forgive yourself, it means you desire to heal, to mature, and to become wiser. If this is you, the absence of learning from your mistakes is a waste of self-forgiveness. Essentially, you will be forgiving yourself, only to commit the same offense against yourself in the future. It nullifies the entire process, similar to an abusive relationship. If your partner is beating you then asking for forgiveness, only to do the same thing the next day or in a week, they need to save their apology. The magic is in the accountability. As in the act of self-forgiveness,

> *The accountability is in the self-correction.*

Forgiveness of God. One of my clients lost his mother over ten years ago due to his stepfather murdering her. Prior to the murder, he had a great relationship with his stepfather. The death of his mother and conviction of his stepfather was devastating as you can imagine, as he felt like he lost both of his parents on the same day. Prior to this tragic experience, this client was God-fearing, prayerful, and a regular churchgoer. During therapy, it was discovered that my client was blaming both himself and God for his losses. He had not had a conversation with God for years and had disassociated himself from his previous church family. During therapy, a major aspect of work was dedicated to redirecting forgiveness. Neither he nor God could be blamed for a decision that was of his stepfather's free will. He also processed a desire to visit his stepfather in prison to seek long-awaited answers to questions. Through the process of self-evaluation, redistribution of responsibility, and exploration of forgiveness, he was able to rekindle his relationship with God and truly heal from his loss. As you can plainly see, the appropriate identification of who to forgive can be the crux of healing.

In the midst of overwhelming pain and anguish, people often direct their anger at their God. This is because people have an expectation of God and when that expectation is not met, it challenges their trust and beliefs. But what if your expectations are inappropriate? I tell couples who are in counseling all the time, do not have expectations for each other that you have not vetted and approved with one another prior to setting. The same advice goes for your expectations of God. In my life, I have felt closest to God during periods of fasting, prayer, and meditation. Prior to questioning your faith, first seek answers, be open to listening, and be ready for the responses you may receive. If you are currently angry with God for whatever reason and it has damaged your relationship, follow these steps to reconnect with your faith.

Seek. There is something astonishing that happens when the combination of prayer and fasting is in play. Deny yourself something significant to help you focus on building your relationship with God, while speaking into the ether. Ask the questions of your heart.

Listen. Sit. Sometimes it is good to unplug from the influences of the world. In today's times, we are constantly stimulated by images, sounds, and sensations that keep us hyper-aroused. It is nearly impossible to hear your inner self or God through the noise. Turn it off so that you can tune in.

Be Ready. You will be surprised when you start to actually receive responses. So much so, that you may not believe them to be true. The results can be intimidating and scare you off. Imagine asking for a million dollars and the next day there is a bag of money on your bed. For some, you may dive into the bag without a second thought. For others such as myself, you may be consumed with thoughts about the responsibility of such as bag.

When I was in my early twenties, I was exploring my faith and distinctly remember a time during fasting and prayer when I was asking for specific answers. In the middle of the process, my phone rang and I simply was not ready for what was on the other end of the phone. So, I denied the answer.

Please do not just pray for answers; also pray for readiness to receive them.

Step #3 Understand the Reason for Forgiveness

Forgive to Let Go. There are two reasons to forgive. One reason is to *forgive so that you can let go*. Remember, forgiveness is simply the release of negative energy attached to an event or person. Forgiveness is not synonymous with friendship. To forgive does not mean to love or like or desire to have in your life. You are granted the authority to simply let go of the negative energy attached to a person. Ironically, doing so releases you from bondage; not them! Forgiving to let someone go is as simple as that. The question then becomes... Can you let go? And if you are choosing to hold on to malice in your heart, what good is that doing for you?

Forgive to Maintain a Relationship. The other reason to forgive, is if you have decided to *maintain a relationship* with the person who did you harm. Always remember, you are the final judge for who you allow in your life. There is no one person who overrides your choice to simply walk away. A *decision* is the only thing that makes a person "family." A blood connection merely makes you related. I need to drive home this point, because some people may be stuck on wanting to maintain an unhealthy relationship with a blood relative because they think it's the best thing to do. Meanwhile, the relationship has been nothing short of draining, with no benefits or rewards in sight.

Some relationships are certainly worth maintaining and others simply exhaust your life-force with no relief for rehydration. Relationships should be a platform for reciprocal energy to be shared. If the relationships you are trying to maintain are lopsided, please evaluate them to determine if you truly need to hold on to them. What are the pros and cons of your troublesome relationships? Are your true reasons for holding on to a toxic relationship your image, embarrassment, insecurity, or lack of self-confidence? If so, which is more important, your image or your happiness and self-fulfillment? In some instances, your sanity is on the line.

If you have decided that you want to maintain a relationship with the person who harmed you, then you must forgive them. I have seen this situation happen with couples quite frequently. I was working with one couple who was trying to recover from infidelity. The wife had an affair with someone and maintained the affair even after the husband found out. The husband would catch his wife cheating, she would apologize and say that it wouldn't happen again, but then the cheating would persist. It was clear that she was not going to end her affair. While working with the husband, it was imperative that he have a complete understanding of the situation and his decision to remain married to his wife. Ultimately, he was choosing to be in a "non-monogamous" relationship. This needed to be clear along with all of the reasons he was choosing to subject himself to this continuous treatment from his wife. Although the husband stated that he wanted to remain in the relationship, he walked around in a constant state of rage. He spewed negative energy throughout the home and towards his wife, who he initiated arguments with frequently.

In this husband's mind, he needed to remain angry with his wife so that he could punish her for her actions. This method of responding to the treatment of his wife fostered division and hostility, and more importantly, it kept him miserable. In other words, he was actually punishing himself. He was not enjoying his relationship and his life was virtually on pause, suspended in a fog of resentment.

In these situations, the misconception is that the perpetrator should not be forgiven because forgiveness is a sign of weakness and an open invitation for the perpetrator to continue with the unwanted behavior. This is marvelously untrue. The issue in these situations is not forgiveness. Rather, it is *accountability*. Accountability means to set expectations and to reliably follow through with the consequences identified for failing to uphold those expectations.

Please do not make the mistake of believing just because you have forgiven someone, they are to no longer be held accountable for their actions. Forgiveness and accountability are two separate activities. In contrast to weakness, forgiveness is a show of strength. The key to changing the behavior of his wife was to forgive her, which again releases him from the bondage of negativity, and to essentially hold her accountable. For this husband, he needed less unforgiveness and more accountability.

Another excuse that I hear frequently when someone is trying to justify maintaining animosity is, "What if I forgive this person and they hurt me again? Then I would have wasted my time and energy." How do I respond? "Whether you choose to remain angry and intentionally avoid having fun **or** you choose to forgive, remain positive, and live your best life, that person can still violate your expectations and potentially hurt your feelings again." If that's the case, the true waste of time is remaining angry about something someone did and allowing it to stop any of your forward progress, because neither your happiness nor sadness will influence another person's behavior. It is always the other person's decision and responsibility to honor your friendship and the expectations set for your relationship.

Chains of Ignorance. Sometimes, we simply do not know any better. Ignorance is the number-one stimulus for capitalism. It keeps people stuck in the cycle of spending their last, only to get money and spend again. Ignorance keeps people trapped under a systematic and self-imposed thumb of oppression. Ignorance is the life blood of the slave master's web of lies. It's the true shackles of a slave.

Ignorance encourages unforgiveness. It is the landing strip for unsophisticated thought driven by imprudent emotions. When we don't know any better, our basic instinct tells us to remain angry and hold onto that debilitating feeling towards a person who caused us harm with vivacity and commitment. Well, now you know better. Once you are aware of the purpose for forgiveness and you have identified the reason for forgiving a person, at that point you need to decide to act and practice letting go. A wise man does not merely have knowledge; he simply exercises that knowledge.

Chains of Pride. In many cases, the only thing in the way of offering forgiveness is *pride*. Please accept that allowing self-pride to stop you from releasing negative energy only prolongs your healing. Self-pride is the barricade in the way of *acceptance* and acceptance is what is required to forgive. You must accept the reality of your current circumstances and know the power that you possess within that set of circumstances. Know that you have the authority to change whether or not you continue to feel unhappy about your situation. If you choose not to exercise your power, then check your pride. Is your pride in the way?

Step #4 Decide!

Once you know the purpose for forgiving, you identified who to forgive, and you have embraced your reason for forgiving, then you need to *decide*. Are you going to remain stagnated in your growth as a person and on your journey to healing, **or** are you going to do whatever it takes to evolve into the well-adjusted, self-aware, emotionally-competent, and time-efficient person you deserve to be? Set all excuses aside and simply make a choice. Remember the formula for being intentional. Do not allow emotions and distorted thinking to get in the way of your intentions. Your healing will depend on it.

Step #5 Let Go!

Now that you have decided to forgive, you made the best choice for your health, your healing, and your future and you need to practice *letting go*. Don't forget, we are always in the process of conditioning or reconditioning ourselves. You may not have realized it, but you have conditioned yourself to either forgive graciously or to hold onto grudges. You have done this over and over again and have reinforced your behavior by telling yourself you are doing the best thing. You have reassured your behavior and have woven it into the fabric of how you operate. So now you may be thinking, "How do I begin to change this part of who I am? It is so deep rooted."

You will need to unlearn how you have previously exercised forgiveness and repeatedly execute this new process. Change is absolutely possible. It requires patience, understanding, and intentionality. You will need to practice letting go every chance you get. It does not matter how small or how big the opportunity. If someone cuts you off in traffic or bumps into you at the grocery store, forgive. If someone takes too long to hit the gas at the light after you have been waiting for quite some time to turn, forgive. If the cashier is taking too long to ring up the groceries and they are cutting into your time, forgive. If your child fails to take out the trash in time, forgive. If your spouse or partner fails to consider you before themselves, forgive. If your pet fails to make it outside before relieving themselves on your floor, forgive.

The key to making this change in your life is to commit to the change in every area of your life. If you fall short at any point, remind yourself of your goal and jump right back in the game. Do not allow setbacks to determine your destination. What do you need to let go?

Chapter Seven
Universal Law

"There is nothing noble in being superior to your fellow man; true nobility is being superior to your former self."

— *Ernest Hemingway*

I need for everyone reading this book to be fully prepared for what you are getting yourself into. There is a universal law that is inescapable.

Whenever we make a definitive decision to change something in our lives, we will surely face adversity and the test will be immediate and of equal measure.

The interesting truth is that the adversity we encounter will be equivalent to the change we are attempting to make. I have experienced this every time I have been intentional about making a change in my life. When discussing change with my clients, I always challenge the nonbelievers to test out this theory. I ask them to decide for themselves something they want to change, and we just sit back and watch as the temptation to do something different pops up out of nowhere. For those who are intentionally practicing abstinence from sex or toxic relationships, old flames who represent the exact types of people they are staying away from will reach out. For those who decided to change their diet, stop smoking cigarettes, or decrease alcohol consumption, opportunities would certainly present themselves to break their fast and indulge in their vices.

I have been following my cholesterol since I was nineteen years old. I was in college, playing football and in the best shape of my life, when my primary-care physician told me that my cholesterol was elevated. I thought that was peculiar given my involvement in rigorous exercise on a daily basis. My doctor gave me a few suggestions to get a handle on it or he would have to prescribe medication for me. At nineteen, hearing the possibility that I would need to be placed on medication made me feel like I was having an out-of-body experience. So, I adjusted my diet by cutting out fried foods, red meat, and minimizing dairy.

Confession: I love fried chicken wings. If you are what you eat, I may have a wing for an arm and a drumstick for a leg. One day, I was leaving my then girlfriend's house to go exercise at the gym. When leaving the gym, I decided to go to the grocery store to grab some fruit and check out the other healthy options.

When you are tested, you will know it, because the temptation will be custom-made for you.

Just the right size, the "choice" shape or color. Whatever your pleasure, your demise will appear in picture-perfect form. It reminds me of the original *Ghost Busters,* when at the end of the movie they had to clear their minds to avoid picking their destruction. In this case, (and I have never seen this before or after this day) as the front doors of the grocery store opened, before I could pass the cash registers or even grab a cart, that all-too-familiar aroma hit my nose as I walked in. There was a woman pulling fresh, golden brown, and extra-crispy chicken wings out of hot grease to drain. By this time in my life, I was well aware of the universal law of adversity. Thus, the second I saw deliciously golden wings with my name written on them, I quickly detoured and made a dash to the "non-diabetes" section. At that point in my life, I was insulted by life's effort to sabotage my good intentions, but I respected the fact that life is reliable when it comes to the tests.

I am still uncovering the secrets of the universal law. What I do know is that there are negative and positive forces in operation all around us at all times. They are at war within us and they are in constant opposition outside of us. Our charge is to be aware of these forces or energies at work and acknowledge that we have influence over them. I am still working to understand our precise authority over them.

At this point, I believe two things happen simultaneously. We have the power to manifest events, people, and tangible items in our lives through the power of thought. I have personally experienced this and know others who have done the same. Therefore, we must be careful of the energy we project. Concurrently, forces outside of us will also place barriers in our lives. I know this to be true because of events such as the fried chicken in the grocery store. I was not focusing any energy on fried chicken when that test happened. That was a test that was generated by outside forces. In either case, we are tasked with the same assignment: Pass the Test!

Remember this: significant change is the sincere embrace of a new lifestyle. Respect the process and do not become discouraged or overwhelmed by the reality that you will have to constantly implement the strategies we have discussed. You are swallowing the red pill which will unlock your illusion of hopelessness, and this will require the demolition and reconstruction of your mind. Nay, a commitment to become a different person which will require devout intention and persistence. Over time, you will adjust to your new subsistence and even then, you will need to continue with your efforts to remain the restored you.

For 14 years, I worked for the federal government in community corrections with men and women suffering from co-occurring mental health and substance-use challenges. Successful cases were scarce; however, the individuals who maintained a clean lifestyle and sobriety all had one thing in common. They remained *plugged-in* to a system or a support network that facilitated positive growth. They were faithful and unwavering. Staying plugged-in is the relentless approach unquestionably required for you to maintain long-term behavior change. What positive and influential network of people are you plugged into?

Here is your chance! This is your calling to the altar. That moment when the pastor has been asking for one more person to come forward for about ten minutes. You have been at the edge of your seat, itching to get up and do something different for quite some time now. If you have reached the end of this book, you may be still procrastinating because halfway through the pages you should have thrown it down and run to pick up the phone to call someone, to go pack your bags, to put in your two-week notice, to schedule that appointment with Dr. E, to go visit that family member or reach out to that friend, to confront your pain face-to-face! Take a look at your life. If you are unhappy about painful circumstances that you can change, please don't complain about it! Get over it! Or ***Run to the Pain***!

EVANS   Run to the Pain

Acknowledgements

To My Queen, Jonvoana R. Evans

AKA Life Coach Von

For many years, I was wandering through the wilderness of life with no compass, no navigation system, no water for hydration, no muse for continuous stimulation, no big game to chase to keep me sharp and motivated to maximize my skills. Until you. As my compass, you provide me with direction. I have a destination and aim for it with every breath. My navigation system, my support, my "tether," providing the comfort and security of a shared journey. You hydrate me and keep me refreshed with energy to go to war on psychological battlefields daily. Your essence, your drive, your passion for life and burning desire to uplift others remains my inspiration. Your relentless effort to amplify your competencies and expand our territory keeps me razor-sharp and powered to be Tag-Team champions! Thank you for being my "bunny rabbit!" T&B

To My Mother, Veltina Evans

I witnessed firsthand the impact of an angel, and how being a blessing to others is ultimately a blessing to one's self. I felt the love shown to you by the people who you cared for and counseled. That spawned a seed in me to be a servant leader. I followed your example and never looked back. Thank you for always being a listening ear. A silent supporter. Unwavering and always true! A shining star for others to marvel! A true gift to the world!

To My First-Born Child, Shawn Evans

The day you were born, I held you in my arms and looked you in the face. I was looking in a mirror. Little did I know, that handheld mirror would change my life forever. All of the pain, the trials, court hearings, custody arrangements, long drives, teacher conferences, football practices, driving lessons, arguments, laughter, and mistakes were worth it. They all molded me into who I am today. We raised each other; you into a Man, and me into a Trailblazer. You have always been on my heels, chasing my strength, accomplishments, and wisdom. And your pursuit has kept me fast, light on my feet, quick and agile. Don't stop coming, and I won't stop leaving a trail ignited by fire and purified by blood, sweat, and tears.

To My Children,

Tamir AKA Mir Mir, TaQara AKA Reezie, TaRheeyn AKA Rheeny Pop, Ryan AKA Cute Poop,

and Roman AKA Romy Rome

Each of you is extremely special, talented, and beautiful. You are all my reasons for pushing to set the best example possible for a human being, a man, an African American man, a husband, a father, and a friend. You all inspire me to be the best version of me. And I will continue to do everything in my power to mold you into the best versions of you. Whether you like it or not! (Shrugs and group hug.)

To My Personal Family

Family is what we choose to make it. Blood or no blood. Those who I have stamped as "friend," qualify as family. Thank you all who have been supportive of my endeavors and who have remained true. I love and appreciate each of you.

To My Professional Family

My clients are my professional family. Each of you has added value to my life and my profession, and you were very influential throughout the journey to complete this book. Thank you for entrusting me with your time, your hearts, your minds, your vulnerabilities, your fears, and your desires. I do not take my responsibility lightly.

References

Anand, KJS, and Craig, K. (1996). New Perspectives on the Definition of Pain. *Pain* vol.67, p.3-6.

Apkarian, A. V., Bushnell, M. C., Treede, R. D., & Zubieta, J. K. (2005). Human brain mechanisms of pain perception and regulation in health and disease. *European Journal of Pain (London, England),* 9(4), 463-484.

Beazley-Long, N., Durrant, A., Swift, M., & Donaldson, L. (2018). The physiological functions of central nervous system pericytes and a potential role in pain. Version 1: referees: 2 approved. *F1000Research*, 7.

De Pascalis, V., Varriale, V., & Cacace, I. (2015). Pain Modulation in Waking and Hypnosis in Women: Event-Related Potentials and Sources of Cortical Activity. *PLoS ONE*, 10(6), 1-38.

Deer, T., Naidu, R., Strand, N., Sparks, D., Abd-Elsayed, Alaa., Kalia, H., Hah, J., Mehta, P., Sayed, D., & Gulati, A. (2020). A review of the bioelectronic implications of stimulation of the peripheral nervous system for chronic pain conditions. *Bioelectronic Medicine*, 6(1), 1-13.

Derbyshire SW. (2010). Foetal Pain? *Best Practice &Research Clinical Obstetrics and Gynaecology*, doi:10.1016/j.bpobgyn.2010.02.013

Guytun, A. (1981, 1986) Textbook of Medical Physiology, sixth edition, WB Saunders Co, p. 611

Lattanzi, R., Maftei, D., Marconi, V., Florenzano, F., Franci, S., Borsani, E., Rodella, L. F., Balboni, G., Salvadori, S., Sacerdote, P., & Negri, L. (2015). Prokineticin 2 Upregulation in the Peripheral Nervous System Has a Major Role in Triggering and Maintaining Neuropathic Pain in the Chronic Constriction Injury Model. *BioMed Research International*, 2015, 1-15.

Lim, M., Roosink, M., Kim, J. S., Kim, H. W., Lee, E. B., Son, K. M., Kim, H. A., & Chung, C. K. (2016). Augmented Pain Processing in Primary and Secondary Somatosensory Cortex in Fibromyalgia: A Magnetoencephalography Study Using Intra-Epidermal Electrical Stimulation. *PLoS ONE*, 11(3), 1-22.

Merskey H. (1991). The definition of pain. *European Psychiatry*; 6:153-59.

Nanay, B. (2017). Pain and Mental Imagery. *Monist, 100*(4), 485-500

Nakata, H., Sakamoto, K., & Kakigi, R. (2014). Meditation reduces pain-related neural activity in the anterior cingulate cortex, insula, secondary somatosensory cortex, and thalamus. *Frontiers in Psychology*, 5, 1489.

Osinki, T., Acapo, S., Bensmail, D., Bouhassira, D., & Martinez, V. (2020). Central Nervous System Reorganization and Pain After Spinal Cord Injury: Possible Targets for Physical Therapy- A Systematic Review of Neuroimaging Studies. *Physical Therapy, 100*(6), 946-962.

Page, S. (2015). The Neoroanatomy and Physiology of Pain Perception in the Developing Human. *Issues in Law & Medicine*, 30(2), 227-236.

Santiago, M., Tumilty, S., Macznik, A., & Mani, R. (2016). Does Acupuncture Alter Pain-related Functional Connectivity of the Central Nervous System? A Systematic Review. *Journal of Acupuncture & Meridian Studies*, 9(4), 167-177.

Seymour, B., & Mancini, F. (2020). Hierarchical models of pain: Inference, information-seeking, and adaptive control. *NeuroImage*, 222.

Shih, H.-C., Kuan, Y.-H., & Shyu, B.-C. (2017). Targeting brain-derived neurotrophic factor in the medial thalamus for the treatment of central poststroke pain in a rodent model. *Pain*, 7, 1302.

Tamaddonfard, E., Erfanparast, A., Ghasemi, H., Henareh-Chareh, F., Hadidi, M., Mirzakhani, N., Seyedin, S., Taati, M., Salighedar, R., Salimi, S., & Safaei, F. (2016). The role of histamine H1, H2 and H3 receptors of ventral posteromedial nucleus of thalamus in modulation of trigeminal pain. *European Journal of Pharmacology*, 791, 696-702. Treede, R. D., Kenshalo, D. R., Gracely, R. H., & Jones, A. K. (1999). The cortical representation of pain. *Pain,* 79(2-3), 105-111

Wu, D., Wang, S., Stein, J., Aziz, T., & Green, A. (2014). Reciprocal interactions between the human thalamus and periaqueductal gray may be important for pain perception. *Experimental Brain Research*, *232*(2), 527-534.

www.ingramcontent.com/pod-product-compliance
Lightning Source LLC
Chambersburg PA
CBHW030912080526
44589CB00010B/263